Foods of
Australia

Barbara Sheen

KIDHAVEN PRESS
A part of Gale, Cengage Learning

Detroit • New York • San Francisco • New Haven, Conn • Waterville, Maine • London

GALE
CENGAGE Learning™

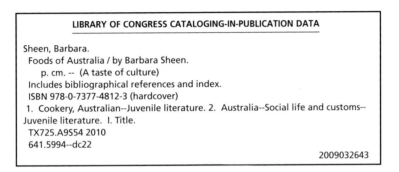

LIBRARY OF CONGRESS CATALOGING-IN-PUBLICATION DATA

Sheen, Barbara.
  Foods of Australia / by Barbara Sheen.
      p. cm. -- (A taste of culture)
  Includes bibliographical references and index.
  ISBN 978-0-7377-4812-3 (hardcover)
  1. Cookery, Australian--Juvenile literature. 2. Australia--Social life and customs--Juvenile literature. I. Title.
  TX725.A9S54 2010
  641.5994--dc22
                                                          2009032643

Kidhaven Press
27500 Drake Rd.
Farmington Hills MI 48331

ISBN-13: 978-0-7377-4812-3
ISBN-10: 0-7377-4812-5

Printed in the United States of America
1 2 3 4 5 6 7 13 12 11 10

Printed by Bang Printing, Brainerd, MN, 1st Ptg., 01/2010

Contents

Chapter 1
Nature's Bounty 4

Chapter 2
Casual Living 17

Chapter 3
Delicious Snacks 29

Chapter 4
Foods for Holidays
and Celebrations 41

Metric Conversions 52

Notes 53

Glossary 55

For Further Exploration 57

Index 59

Picture Credits 63

About the Author 64

Nature's Bounty

Australia is unique among nations in that it spans a whole continent. It is the sixth-largest country in the world, and it is blessed with a mild climate, fertile soil, rich grazing lands, 22,812 miles (36,712km) of coastland, and an abundance of inland waterways. These natural resources provide the Australian people with a huge supply of delicious foods. Beef, lamb, seafood, and fruit are among their favorites.

A Meat Lover's Paradise

Australians eat a lot of meat. They have been raising sheep and cattle since the British first colonized the continent in 1788. Australia's first European settlers were men and women convicted of crimes in England.

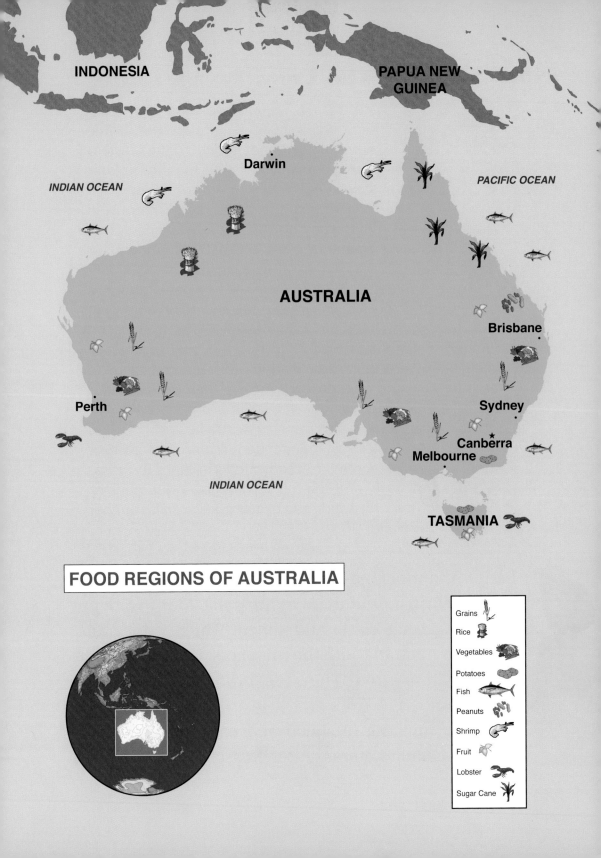

INDONESIA

PAPUA NEW GUINEA

Darwin

INDIAN OCEAN

PACIFIC OCEAN

AUSTRALIA

Brisbane

Perth

Sydney

Canberra

Melbourne

INDIAN OCEAN

TASMANIA

FOOD REGIONS OF AUSTRALIA

Grains

Rice

Vegetables

Potatoes

Fish

Peanuts

Shrimp

Fruit

Lobster

Sugar Cane

The Land Down Under

Australia is called "The Land Down Under," because it is located below the equator. It was not known to the Western world until 1606 when a Spanish explorer sailed within sight of the continent.

Europeans showed little interest in Australia until 1768 when British explorer James Cook landed here. He claimed possession of the continent for Great Britain.

The British decided to use Australia as a penal colony, a place to send convicts. Between 1788 and 1853 more than 150,000 convicts were sent to Australia. These men and women were put to work. Most served only four years, then they were put on probation. This allowed them to earn money, and own property before their sentence was up. Many became wealthy. In the 19th century other British and Asian settlers also came to Australia.

Today Australia is an independent nation that governs itself. Queen Elizabeth II of the United Kingdom is Australia's head of state, and she has certain governing powers. A governor-general appointed by the queen carries out her duties in Australia.

Rather than locking them up in overcrowded English jails, the British sent them to Australia. Many were put to work raising cattle and sheep, which were transported to Australia with the prisoners. By 1793 free settlers began to arrive. They, too, brought livestock with them.

Today millions of sheep and cattle are raised on ranches called stations. After Russia, Australia raises

more sheep than any other nation in the world. Its sheep flock numbers about 170,000 million. Australia also boasts the world's largest **cattle station**. It measures about 6 million acres (2.4 million ha), making it four times larger than the biggest ranch in the United States.

Australian beef and lamb are world famous for their good taste and high quality. Because Australian farmers let their cattle graze on grasses instead of feeding them grain, Australian beef is leaner and contains less fat and cholesterol than American beef. Steak is prob-

Meat is an important part of Australian cooking and lamb is a staple. Australia raises more sheep than any other nation in the world, after Russia.

Aussie Burger with the Lot

Burgers are a popular meat dish in Australia. Australians like their burgers with lots of toppings. They prefer a hard roll to a soft bun.

Ingredients

1 uncooked hamburger patty
1 onion slice
1 beet slice
1 tomato slice
1 pineapple ring
1 cheese slice
1 bacon slice, cooked
1 small lettuce leaf
ketchup to taste
1 hard round roll large enough for a hamburger, cut in half and toasted

Instructions

1. Put the burger in a nonstick frying pan or on a hot grill. Cook the burger until the bottom is browned, then flip the burger. The burger is done when it is no longer pink inside.
2. Put ketchup to taste on the bottom half of the roll. Add the burger.
3. Pile all the other ingredients on top. Many Australians also add a fried egg.
4. Cover with the other half of the roll. Enjoy!

Serves 1.

ably the most popular beef dish here. Veal or calf meat is also quite popular. Farmers usually feed their Australian calves milk. This makes the meat melt-in-the-

Australian Wildlife

Australia is the home of a variety of animals. Its isolation from other continents has given its wildlife a unique character. Marsupials, mammals that are born not fully developed and are carried in a mother's pouch, are the most common native mammals here. These include kangaroos, possums, and wallabies, small animals that resemble kangaroos. Australia also has mammals called monotremes that lay eggs. The duck-billed platypus is such an animal.

Australia is also the home to many different snakes, including the highly poisonous taipan and death adder. Saltwater crocodiles live here too.

Australia is also the home of many different birds. The kookaburra is a common bird that sounds like it is laughing. Emus, tall birds that cannot fly, are also native birds.

Other animals live in Australia's rain forest. It is the home of hundreds of different varieties of butterflies, frogs, and birds.

Australia has many unique animals. Marsupials are the most common native mammals.

mouth tender.

Farmers frequently feed Australian lambs with milk, too. Few Australians can resist its delicate flavor. With the exception of New Zealanders and Mongolians, Australians eat more lamb than any other group.

Australians prepare lamb in a lot of different ways. Lamb is roasted, barbecued, fried, baked, and broiled. It is slow cooked in hearty stews, pounded into thin, batter-dipped cutlets, and smothered with spicy curry sauce in dishes that Indian immigrants brought to Australia. It is ground into sausages, or **snags**; marinated in soy sauce and vinegar; cooked with pineapple; and added to earthy casseroles. Lamb roast has been a traditional Sunday dinner ever since Australia was colonialized. And, grilled lamb chops are a national favorite. According to Australian chef Graeme Newman, "all countries have their own special and distinct aromas. Australia's is of sizzling lamb chops."[1]

Bountiful Fish and Seafood

Fish and seafood are also wildly popular in Australia. Most Australians live close to the coast, and freshly caught seafood is a delicious staple of their diet. Australia's coastal waters and inland waterways teem with life. The world's largest reef system, the Great Barrier Reef, is located off the coast of north-

east Australia. It is the home of more than 1,500 species of fish. Still more edible water creatures are found in Australia's other waters. "If you are lucky you can catch lobster or crabs, scrape oysters or mussels off the rocks

Fish and seafood are another important staple in Australian cooking. Australians love to eat barramundi, a fish that is caught wild but is cultivated on fish farms.

or pick up a kilo or two of prawns [extra large shrimp] at the co-op [a food store] for a feast,"[2] explains Life-Tips, a Web site offering tips about Australia.

Australians have a huge array of seafood to choose from. Some, such as shark, trout, crabs, oysters, clams, scallops, tuna, and salmon, are familiar to Americans. Others have odd-sounding names like **Moreton Bay bugs**, **yabbies**, **prawns**, and **barramundi** (bar-a-mund-i).

Moreton Bay bugs are not bugs at all. They are small, sweet lobsters that Australians like to steam and cover with butter, or toss in a cold seafood platter. Yabbies are freshwater crayfish. They look and taste like tiny lobsters.

Prawns are extra-large, sweet, and juicy shrimp. Grilled, fried, or boiled and served with lemon and hot melted butter, they are an Australian favorite. Prawns are so popular that the Australian town of Ballina, which is located at the mouth of the Richmond River, a popular prawn-fishing site, welcomes visitors with a giant pink prawn perched above the town's entrance. Typically seafood shops in this prawn fishing community sell more than 2,500 pounds (1,134kg) of prawns per week.

Other fish, such as barramundi, are less familiar. It is a sweet, moist, buttery white fish that Australians adore. They grill it, broil it, and cook it in stews and casseroles. They dust it with flour and fry it until it is golden. And, they eat it raw in sushi. Australian ce-

Toad-in-the-Hole

This is a popular Australian meat dish. Australians usually use lamb sausage but any type of thin breakfast sausage will work. Australians like to top this with thin tomato sauce similar to ketchup or brown gravy.

Ingredients
8–12 brown-and-serve link sausages
2 eggs, beaten
1 cup milk
1 cup self-rising flour
1 tablespoon cooking oil
salt and pepper to taste

Instructions
1. Preheat the oven to 400°F.
2. Combine the flour, milk, eggs, and salt and pepper. Mix well, beating out any lumps. The batter should be the consistency of heavy cream. Let the mixture sit for ten minutes.
3. Pour the oil into a baking pan. Arrange the sausages in rows in the pan. Bake until the oil is very hot, about ten minutes.
4. Carefully remove the pan from the oven. Pour in the batter. Try not to completely cover the sausage.
5. Bake for 30–45 minutes, until the dough is puffy and golden.
Serves 4.

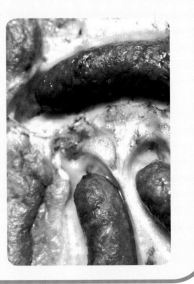

Toad-in-the-Hole is a popular Australian meat dish.

lebrity chef Luke Mangan explains, "I've served barramundi to thousands of people around the world and it's always a huge hit!"[3]

Although barramundi is caught wild, the fish is also cultivated on fish farms. Australian **aquaculture**, or fish farming, is a large industry, which takes health and environmental issues seriously. Raising barramundi on fish farms ensures that the wild population is not depleted. And, since the water that the fish are raised in is purified and recycled constantly, the fish not only taste delicious, but they are also not exposed to mercury or other waterborne pollutants. It is no wonder that *Bon Appetite* magazine named barramundi as one of its top-50 "green" foods.

Sumptuous Fruits

Australian fruit also tastes terrific. Juicy fruit of every size, shape, and color grow in abundance in Australia's mild climate. Australian cooks take full advantage of the vast variety of fruits at their fingertips. According to Australian chef Tony Baker, "the whole range of citrus—limes and mandarins, and countless acres of oranges are arrayed across the southeast Australian heartland. Berry fruits, grapes eaten fresh or dried into raisins . . . apricots and peaches, likewise fresh and dried, giant watermelons . . . mangoes, pineapples, pears, and apples . . . abound."[4]

Those are just the more familiar fruits. There is also a seemingly endless assortment of exotic tropical fruits. **Passion fruit** is a local favorite. Australians turn the

Fresh fruit grows in abundance in Australia because of its mild climate. The vast variety of fruit includes oranges, berries, watermelon, and exotic tropical fruits such as passion fruit.

jellylike orange pulp of this incredibly fragrant fruit into ice cream and sorbet. They use it in cheesecake and add it to fruit salad where its slightly tart taste enhances the flavor of the other fruits. And, they peel it and eat it fresh. New York City chef Melissa Plotkin recalls her first experience eating passion fruit in Australia: "I'd never really seen one before. After smelling and tasting one, then another and another, I was hooked."[5]

There are also black sapotes that taste and smell like chocolate pudding and starchy breadfruit, which is cooked like a potato and tastes like fresh baked bread. Thanks to Chinese settlers, who came to Australia in the late 1800s with banana plants in tow, there are bananas in a rainbow of colors. Yellow, blue, green, and red-skinned bananas are all grown here.

The list of fruits goes on and on. Australians eat them fresh, blend them with milk in sweet and creamy smoothies, and add them to curries and sweet and sour dishes. They grill them with meat; transform them into juices and icy desserts; bake them in pies, cakes, and breads; dip them in chocolate sauce; use them in place of vegetables; and combine them with vegetables in crunchy, sweet, and savory salads.

The abundance of fresh fruit in addition to so many other foods provides Australians with a seemingly endless feast. Fresh seafood and fish, fork-tender lamb and beef, and luscious juicy fruit are as much a part of Australian cooking as they are a part of the nation's history and character.

Casual Living

Australia's mild weather makes it possible for Australians to enjoy the outdoors year-round. Cooking and eating outdoors is part of this fun. Almost every home has a backyard barbecue, or **barbie** as it is known in Australia. Even urban dwellers have small barbies on their balconies. Parks, beaches, roadside rest stops, and picnic areas throughout the nation have public barbies. There are even restaurants in which diners barbecue their own meals. Chef Melissa Plotkin recalls,

> Most people lead a casual, very unfussy lifestyle. In fact, one of the restaurants I went to was a "grill your own" type place. It was a casual, yet lovely eatery with two large open grills in the cor-

Almost every Australian home has a backyard barbecue, or barbie, and grilling is done year round.

ners of the dining room and a big outdoor seating area. There was a meat/fish counter where you order your protein and then you season and cook it yourself.[6]

A Long History

Throwing some meat or seafood on the barbie is considered a way of life in Australia. "Every person who claims to be a 'true blue' [native-born] Aussie (Authentic Aussie) MUST have a Barbie,"[7] chefs Betsey and Graeme Newman insist.

Australians have been cooking outdoors for a long

time. Long before the British arrived, Australian **Aborigines**, the continent's first inhabitants, cooked native animals like kangaroos, wild goats, and emus over an open fire. They combined the meat with native fruits and vegetables such as wild oranges, plums, and yams. This became known as bush food, or **bush tucker**.

Nineteenth-century Australian cattlemen and shepherds cooked most of their meals outdoors too. They heated beans and liquids and made damper, a simple bread, in a tin can known as a **billy**. Like the Aborigines they cooked over a campfire. For these early people, cooking outdoors was a necessity. For modern Australians it is a way to embrace their past while having fun.

Outback Cooking

The Australian outback is the remote wild land far from Australian cities. Also known as the bush, or bushland, the outback takes up four-fifths of the Australian continent. Because it is so vast, the outback is home to many different edible plants and animals. Aborigines lived off these animals and plants for centuries. Settlers in the outback ate both native foods, known as bush tucker, and food they brought with them, such as flour, tea, beef, and lamb.

Many modern Australian chefs are incorporating native Australian foods into their dishes. There are even farms on which crocodiles, emus, and kangaroos are raised for food. Hunting kangaroos for food is also popular in parts of Australia. Kangaroo meat is a favorite food here. It is lean and is eaten like steak and in stews.

"There's nothing better than a barbie on a hot Australian summer day," says Australian food writer, Priscilla Cox. "Your mates [friends], backyard cricket. . . . It's awesome being Australian."[8]

Strings of Snags

It should come as no surprise that many of the Australian people's favorite dishes are cooked on a barbie. Australians like the smoky flavor and the tantalizing aroma that barbecuing adds to food.

Barbecued snags, steaks, and prawns are among everyone's favorites. Snags are sausages that are strung together on long strings, which can be cut apart. They are usually made of lamb, but can also be made of beef or pork. Generally, they are shorter and fatter than American hot dogs.

Many favorite Australian dishes are cooked on a barbie, including snags, which are sausages that are strung together on long strings.

Damper

Damper is a traditional Australian bread. In the past it was made over a campfire either in a billy can or by wrapping the dough around a green stick, and cooking the stick over the fire. Damper can also be baked in an oven. This recipe provides directions for making damper in an oven.

Ingredients
2 cups all-purpose flour
1 cup milk
1/4 teaspoon salt
1 teaspoon sugar
2 tablespoons butter or margarine
1 teaspoon baking soda

Instructions
1. Preheat oven to 375°F.
2. Combine the flour, salt, and baking soda.
3. Mix in the butter, forming fine crumbs.
4. Mix in the milk to make a soft dough.
5. Put the dough on a cutting board dusted with flour. Knead the dough until it is smooth.
6. Spray a round cake pan with nonstick spray. Lightly dust the bottom of the pan with flour.
7. Form the dough into a round loaf. Make a square cut across the top. Put it in the cake pan.
8. Bake 35–40 minutes or until the outside is golden and a fork inserted into the bread comes out dry.

Makes 1 loaf.

Australian Potato Salad

Australians like salad. Potato salad often accompanies barbecued meats and seafood.

Ingredients

4 medium to large potatoes, peeled and cut into chunks
3 hardboiled eggs, sliced
2 slices of cooked bacon chopped or 1/4 cup bacon bits
1/2 onion, minced
1 tablespoon olive oil
1 tablespoon vinegar
1/3 cup mayonnaise
1 teaspoon chopped chives
salt and pepper to taste

Instructions

1. Put the potatoes in a pot with enough water so the potatoes are covered. Bring to a boil. Reduce heat to low. Cover the pot and let the potatoes cook slowly until they are tender, about 10–15 minutes. Drain the water from the pot. Let the potatoes cool for 15–30 minutes.
2. In a large bowl mix the oil, vinegar, eggs, onions, chives, bacon, and potatoes. Then add the mayonnaise and mix well.
3. Put the potato salad in the refrigerator to chill for one hour.

Serves 4.

Snags, or any other food cooked on a barbie, are usually prepared by the man of the house. In Australia

barbecuing is considered a manly activity and barbecuing is a common male hobby. According to chef Tony Baker, "when two Australian men stop talking about sports, there is a good chance they are busy swapping their secret recipes for the perfect marinade."[9]

Snags are cooked on a flat grill plate. Most Australian barbies do not have grates. For this reason the snags do not get the grill lines that Americans usually have on their barbecued food. Mounds of sweet grilled onions, which are cooked on the barbie before the meat, almost always accompany snags. The lady of the house prepares other side dishes, such as a green salad, fruit salad, or potato salad. Or, side dishes may be brought by guests, many of whom may be neighbors drawn by the irresistible aroma.

Juicy Steaks and Prawns

Barbecued steak is another Australian favorite. Not just any steak will do. Australians like their steaks thick, lean, and tender. Australian chefs often cut a small flap or pocket in the steak, which they stuff with any number of ingredients. Mushrooms and onions are popular; so are sliced bananas. Steaks stuffed with bananas are often topped with golden rings of grilled pineapple. The fruit adds a surprisingly sweet flavor to the meat, which Australians prefer cooked thoroughly, or well-done.

French fries, which Australians call **chips**, often accompany steak. Other meats are also often served with steak. A mixed grill is a very popular dish in Australia.

Barbecued prawns (shrimp) are another popular favorite of Australians.

It consists of steak, snags, and lamb chops. These are all cooked on a barbie along with bacon, mushrooms, onions, and sliced tomatoes. While the steaks and chops are cooking, they may be brushed with a sauce made of beer, vinegar, and Worcestershire sauce. The sauce makes the already tender meat as soft as butter and adds an earthy spiciness to the flavor. Before the sizzling meat is served, the cook piles the mushrooms on top of the steaks. The lamb chops are adorned with crispy slices of bacon. The tomatoes, onions, and snags are served on the side.

International Influences

Immigrants from all over the world have made Australia their home, and they have influenced Australian cooking. For instance, the city of Melbourne has the third-largest Greek-speaking population in the world. There are many Greek restaurants here. And, Greek-style cooking, which uses olive oil in place of butter and adds spices such as garlic to food, has influenced modern Australian cooks. In the past, Australians rarely used garlic and cooked with butter rather than oil.

Australia also has a large Asian population. Chinese immigrants arrived here in the late 19th century, during Australia's gold rush. Sweet and sour dishes, which are a Chinese favorite, are quite popular in Australia. Australians also cook and eat curries and sushi, which were brought to the nation by Indian and Japanese settlers. And, Thai restaurants are wildly popular too.

And, for those times when Australians prefer seafood, there are barbecued prawns. They may be brushed with lemon juice and melted butter and slipped onto the barbie. Or, they may be threaded on skewers with chunks of pineapple, mushrooms, and onions. Either way, the results are irresistible—tender, white, sweet, and juicy. It is no wonder they are a popular favorite.

Takeaway Favorites

When Australians do not feel like barbecuing but still want to eat outdoors, they purchase takeaway foods.

Fish-and-chips shops are very popular in Australia. A plate of fish and chips is served in a paper cone at the Elizabeth Street Pier in Hobart, Tasmania, Australia.

These are dishes that are cooked in specialty shops for Australians to eat at picnic tables outside the shops, in parks, or at nearby beaches. Takeaway shops are informal. They offer simple dishes that Australians love. Fish-and-chips, an English meal that Australians have adopted as their own, is among everyone's favorite.

Fish-and-chips shops are so popular that in many Australian towns there is at least one shop on every street. The menu is usually posted on a chalkboard. Customers go up to the counter and select the type of fish they prefer. Choices vary depending on what fish are caught in local waters. But flake, the name of a type of shark meat, is found on almost every menu. It is tender and flaky, hence the name.

No matter what type of fish diners select, it is always very fresh. In fact, in some coastal communities, fish-and-chips shops are located so close to the docks that fishermen unload their latest catches right into the shops.

The fish may be breaded with a thick batter made from flour and beer or simply be dusted with bread crumbs. Either way, it is deep-fried in hot bubbling oil until it is golden. The chips, which are three times wider than American French fries, are never frozen like many American fast-food fries. They are made fresh, which gives them a nice dense texture.

Once the fish-and-chips are fried to perfection, they are packed in a thick sheet of paper. This keeps the fish-and-chips hot and moist. Australians sprinkle salt on top, as well as vinegar or sweet and spicy Thai chili

sauce. According to chefs Betsey and Graeme Newman, "there's nothing like a pack of hot fish and chips with plenty of salt."[10]

For Australians, there is nothing like eating their favorite foods outdoors. Foods like fish-and-chips and barbecued steaks, snags, and prawns blend well with the Australian people's fun-loving lifestyle. These dishes bring to mind warm days filled with friends and fun. It is no wonder these foods are among Australia's favorites.

Delicious Snacks

Australians like to snack. Most take a morning tea break. But it does not have to be teatime for Australians to enjoy a sweet or savory snack.

Morning Tea

Like their English ancestors, Australians love tea. As a nation, they drink 15.5 million cups of the steaming beverage, which they drink with milk, every day.

Most Australians take a tea break at 11 A.M. Many schools and businesses sound a bell or a whistle at this time. All work stops and everyone enjoys about a twenty-minute break during which they relax and reenergize over a cup of tea and a snack. Students and workers may bring tea and a snack from home or

Macadamia Nuts

Macadamia nuts are native to Australia. They grow on small evergreen trees in the rain forests of eastern Australia. Long before the British arrived in Australia, the Aborigines made these rich-tasting nuts a part of their diet.

Macadamia nuts are very nutritious. They are a good source of protein, fiber, calcium, potassium, and other vital minerals. They can be eaten raw or roasted. Macadamia oil can be used in cooking, and chocolate-covered macadamia nuts are a delicious treat.

The first Australian macadamia nut plantation was established in 1880. Today the macadamia nut industry is one of Australia's largest industries.

The macadamia nut is native to Australia.

purchase them at the **canteen**, or cafeteria, at their school or business. Some Australians also take a late afternoon tea break. Since it is not typically scheduled into the work day, afternoon tea is most popular on the weekends.

Australians are very particular about how tea is made. First they pour boiling water into a teapot to

warm the pot. Once the pot is warm, they pour out the water and drop in one teabag or one teaspoon of loose tea per person. Next they add fresh boiling water to the pot. They do not reboil water because this gives the tea a metallic taste. Once the tea has steeped, the teabags are removed. Or, if loose tea was used, a strainer is placed over the top of the pot, to catch the leaves as the tea is poured.

Biscuits and Scones

Biscuits and **scones** (sconz) are perfect snacks with morning tea. Americans might find these names confusing—Australians call all types of cookies "biscuits," while "scones" are what Americans call biscuits. Scones may be plain, or they may be filled with raisins, pine-

Tim Tams are store bought cookies that are an Australian favorite. The cookie consists of two crunchy chocolate covered wafers layered over a choice of fillings.

apple, or other fruit. They are served warm with butter or cool with a range of jellies and a dollop of whipped cream. But, no matter what they contain or what they are topped with, Australians like their scones light and fluffy.

Like in America, there are many different types of Australian biscuits (cookies). Most Australians keep tins filled with both homemade and store-bought biscuits. Tim Tams are among the most popular. These store-bought cookies consist of two crunchy, chocolate-covered wafers layered over a choice of fillings. There is chocolate cream, chewy caramel, orange jelly, and vanilla toffee, to name a few. Australians like to "slam" Tim Tams. To do this, they bite off the opposite ends of the cookie, place one bitten end in their tea, and then suck tea through the other bitten end until the Tim Tam is nearly soaked. Then they "slam" the cookie into their mouths before it falls apart. Colin, who attended college in Australia, explains,

I'll never forget Tim Tams, which is one of the greatest cookies because of the Tim Tam slam. To slam one, you take two small bites on diagonally opposite sides so it essentially becomes a straw. Then you sip from a hot beverage until the drink reaches your mouth. By this time, the cookie is melting so you have to eat the rest and it's essentially a warm chocolate wafer cookie. Describing it does not do it justice.[11]

Australian English

Although Australians speak English, they have many words and phrases that may be confusing to other English speakers. Many of these have to do with food. Here are a few:

bacon rasher: A slice of bacon.

bangers: Sausages.

biscuit: A cookie.

brekkie: Breakfast.

chewie: Chewing gum.

chips: Fried potatoes.

chockie: Chocolate.

chook: Chicken.

conserve: Jelly.

crisps: Potato chips.

cut lunch: A packed lunch.

dinnies: Dinner.

elevenses: A name for morning tea.

esky: A portable cooler for storing food or drinks.

fairy floss: Cotton candy.

goog: An egg.

jelly: Jello.

lollies: All types of candies.

mash: Mashed potatoes.

pikelet: A small ready-made pancake.

sammie, or sanger: A sandwich.

scone: A biscuit.

tucker: All food.

Patriotic Biscuits

ANZAC biscuits are another teatime favorite. They have an interesting history. ANZAC is an acronym for the Australian New Zealand Army Corps for whom these hard cookies were first created. Troops from Australia and New Zealand fought in Gallipoli, Turkey, during World War I. The ships that carried food to these men lacked refrigeration and took more than two months to reach them. Food spoilage was a big problem.

Worried that the troops were not getting proper nutrition, a group of Australian women created hearty oat biscuits, which did not spoil easily, to send to them. The biscuits were made with oats, flour, coconut, sugar, boiling water, baking soda, and golden syrup, a honeylike sweetener made from sugar cane, which held the biscuits together.

Veterans march in the ANZAC Day Parade, which is held every year in Australia on April 25 to honor the country's war veterans.

ANZAC Biscuits

ANZAC biscuits are not difficult to make. They should be stored in an airtight container.

Ingredients
1 cup uncooked oatmeal (not instant) or rolled oats
1 cup all-purpose flour
1 cup unsweetened coconut
3/4 cup sugar
1/2 cup butter
1 teaspoon baking soda
2 tablespoons honey
2 tablespoons boiling water

Instructions
1. Preheat the oven to 350°F.
2. Put the honey, baking soda, butter, sugar, and boiling water in a microwave safe bowl. Mix well. Microwave until the mixture boils.
3. Combine the coconut, flour, and oats in a large bowl. Add the liquid mixture. Mix well.
4. Spray two cookie sheets with nonstick spray. Place spoonfuls of the mixture on the cookie sheet about 3 inches apart.
5. Bake about 10–15 minutes, or until the biscuits are golden brown. Cool before eating.

Makes 24 biscuits.

ANZAC biscuits, which are crispy buttery cookies, are a teatime favorite.

The biscuits, which were originally named "Soldiers' Biscuits," were packed in airtight tea tins and shipped to the fighting men. They proved to be so successful that for the rest of the war women throughout Australia and New Zealand devoted themselves to baking them for the troops.

These crispy buttery cookies are still popular today. In fact, if Australia had a national cookie, the ANZAC biscuit would be it. ANZAC biscuits can be purchased in supermarkets and bakeries all over Australia. They are also a homemade specialty. They are especially popular on April 25—ANZAC Day, which is the day Australians honor all their war veterans. According to Woz, the creator of the Aussie Slang Web site, ANZAC biscuits "have won the heart of Aussies the globe over."[12]

Delectable Cakes

While biscuits and scones almost always accompany morning tea, cake is often served with afternoon tea. Australians bake lots of different types of cakes. Slices are among their favorites. These are single layer, rectangular or square cakes topped with a thin layer of icing. The varieties and combinations of cakes and frosting are endless. A banana slice, for example, is made of sweet, moist banana cake crowned with lemon cinnamon frosting. The aroma is almost as enticing as the taste. There are also chocolate marshmallow slices, nut slices, and passion-fruit slices, to name just a few.

Lamingtons are another wildly popular treat. They

Slices of cake are an Australian favorite. The slices are typically single layer, rectangular or square cakes topped with a thin layer of icing.

are cubes of sponge cake coated in chocolate frosting and rolled in coconut. They look like fuzzy marshmallows but taste like cake. They are often served with strawberry jam and whipped cream. The result is wonderfully sweet, rich, and satisfying.

Lamingtons are said to be named after Baron Lamington who was the governor of the Australian state of Queensland at the turn of the 20th century. The

Lamingtons

Lamingtons are not difficult to make, but they can be messy to make.

Ingredients

1 pound sponge or yellow cake
2 cups sugar
1/3 cup unsweetened cocoa powder
1/2 cup milk
2 teaspoons butter or margarine
2 cups unsweetened shredded coconut

Instructions

1. Cut the cake into about 4-inch squares.
2. Mix the sugar and cocoa together in a bowl.
3. Heat the milk and butter in a pan until the butter is melted.
4. Slowly add the milk and butter mixture to the sugar and cocoa. Stir as you add the liquid. The icing should be a thick fluid but not runny.
5. Spread the coconut on a large plate.
6. Cover a cookie sheet with nonstick foil.
7. Using a fork, dip each cake square into the icing. Hold over the icing bowl to allow excess liquid to drip off. Then roll each square in the coconut or sprinkle the coconut onto the square.
8. As each Lamington is coated, put it on the cookie sheet to dry.

Makes 15 to 20 Lamingtons.

Lamingtons are cubes of sponge cake coated in chocolate frosting and rolled in coconut.

cake is so popular that Australians celebrate National Lamington Day annually on July 21.

Savory Pastries

Sweet pastries are not the only type of snack Australians clamor for. Savory little meat pies are another favorite treat. They are an Australian's favorite fast-food. Australians eat over 250 million of them a year. Made with a thin flaky crust, the pies are about 4 inches (10cm) in diameter and are filled with a thick mixture of meat, vegetables, and gravy. Steak and kidney pie and pies with ground meat and mashed potatoes or mashed peas are popular choices. The pies are eaten by hand,

Meat pies are an Australian's favorite fast-food. They are filled with meat, vegetables, and gravy and topped with tomato sauce.

much like a sandwich. So it is important that the filling be thick enough not to drip out. Sometimes meat pies are served floating in green-pea soup. This is called a meat pie floater. Floaters are eaten with a spoon. Australians top the pies with tomato sauce, which is very similar to American ketchup.

Meat pies are especially popular at sporting events where they are the food of choice. Just as Americans eat hot dogs at baseball games, Australians nosh on meat pies at cricket and football matches. "Meat pies," explains Australian food writer Syrie Wongkaew, "are about as Australian as you can get."[13]

Indeed yummy meat pies, chocolatey Lamingtons, sweet milky tea, crunchy biscuits, and creamy slices are all Australian specialties. It is no wonder Australians like to snack. Such delectable treats are hard to resist.

4

Foods for Holidays and Celebrations

Holidays and special occasions give Australians a chance to get together with family and friends, have fun, and enjoy special foods.

Christmas in the Summer

Christmas is a festive time in Australia. Since Australia is located in the Southern Hemisphere, Christmas falls in the summer here, which affects the way Australians celebrate the holiday. For instance, since many Australians spend a lot of time on the beach at this time of year, Father Christmas, the Australian version of Santa Claus, is said to make his rounds in a boat, or even on water skis, rather than in a sleigh.

Christmas foods, too, have a unique Australian twist.

Aboriginal Culture

Australian Aborigines have inhabited Australia for more than 60,000 years. They traveled to Australia over a land bridge from Indonesia during the last Ice Age. They lived in about 600 different groups called clans, similar to Native American tribes. Each clan had its own territory.

The Aborigines were hunter-gatherers. They did not raise crops. They had a great deal of respect for nature and sought to preserve the land they lived on. They had elaborate creation stories known as Dreaming or Dream Time. These stories set up rules about how people should behave.

British settlers drove many Aborigines from their land. When the Aborigines fought back, they were killed. Many others caught diseases from the British settlers and died. The British forced those who remained onto reservations and into church missions. Today many Aborigines live in the Australian outback as well as in Australian towns. They live much like other Australians.

Like their English ancestors, Australians make special Christmas treats. Many Australians start preparing seasonal sweets a week or two before Christmas, so they can have plenty of treats on hand for guests who drop-in for afternoon tea during the week leading up to Christmas. White Christmas is one such treat. Although it hardly ever snows in Australia, and never during December, White Christmas gives Australians a taste of a traditional snowy Christmas. To make White Christ-

mas, cooks combine crispy rice cereal, dried tropical fruit, and shredded coconut and top it with a coat of melted white chocolate. When the mixture cools, Australians have a rich, sweet, crunchy treat.

Pavlova is another holiday favorite. Pavlova is a tall, elegant, lighter-than-air dessert. It is made from **meringue** (mer-rang), a shell-like confection made by combining egg whites and sugar. Pavlova is time-consuming to make, but worth the effort. To make it, cooks beat egg whites until they form firm, stiff peaks. Then they fold in sugar, corn flour

Pavlova was created for Anna Pavlova, a Russian ballerina who visited Australia in the late 1920s.

Pavlova is a holiday favorite. It is made from meringue and typically topped with creamy whipped cream and juicy strawberries.

Australian Meals

Most Australians eat three meals a day. Breakfast is usually eaten early because people like to start their day before the heat rises. It is likely to be dried whole-wheat cereal with milk and honey, or oatmeal with butter and honey, or toast and jam. It is almost always accompanied with a cup of tea.

Lunch is likely to be a sausage roll, which is sausage encased in puff pastry, or a sandwich. Australians make sandwiches out of almost everything. A baked bean sandwich or a cold spaghetti sandwich is not unusual.

Dinner is the largest meal of the day. It is also called tea. But it is not to be confused with morning or afternoon tea, which are snacks. Dinner is usually a hot meal that includes meat or fish and two vegetables.

Australians usually eat three meals a day. Sandwiches are very popular at lunchtime and can be made out of almost anything, including baked beans.

(or cornstarch), vanilla, and vinegar. The mixture is slowly baked for about two hours. The result is a dome-shaped delicacy with a sweet, crisp, outer crust surrounding a soft, creamy, marshmallow-like interior,

which melts in the mouth. Pavlova is usually topped with smooth creamy whipped cream and juicy ripe strawberries. At Christmas, crushed Peppermint Crisps (chocolate candy bars with a hard peppermint filling) are also a popular topping.

Pavlova was created as a tribute to Anna Pavlova, a Russian ballerina who visited Australia in the late 1920s. She is considered to be the greatest ballerina of her time. Her movements and leaps were so astounding that her fans said she floated as if she had wings.

Both Australia and New Zealand claim credit for inventing the dessert. Although it is unclear who created it, one thing is certain, Pavlova is as light and airy as the dancer it was named for. It is, according to chef Shuna Fish Lydon, "an edible translation of sugar turned into a cumulous cloud."[14]

Christmas Pudding the Australian Way

Christmas dinner in Australia is also unique. What is served varies. It may be a traditional lamb roast, or a turkey dinner. But it is also likely to be meat cooked on a barbie or a meal of cold meats eaten on the beach. Indeed, because the weather in late December can reach 100°F (38°C) in parts of Australia, a cold dinner is very popular. But no matter the main course, it is customary to end the meal with Christmas pudding.

Christmas pudding is an English custom. Traditionally it is made of dried fruits; nuts; bread crumbs; and flour moistened with juice or brandy, an alcoholic beverage, and steamed for about eight hours. Cooks hide

In Australia, Christmas dinner usually ends with Christmas pudding, which is tweaked to match the warm weather. It is served cold and Australians typically add ice cream and fresh fruit.

Salad Roll

A salad roll is a popular Australian sandwich. Basically, it is a salad on a roll. So it is a great meal for vegetarians. You can add or subtract sandwich fillings depending on your taste.

Ingredients
2 hard rolls, sliced in half
Butter or margarine
2 beet slices, cut in thin rounds
2 tomato slices, cut in thin rounds
2 teaspoons shredded carrot
2 cucumber slices, cut in thin rounds and peeled
2 orange slices, cut in thin rounds and peeled
2 teaspoons chopped sweet onion
2 lettuce leaves
salt and pepper to taste

Instructions
1. Spread the rolls with a thick layer of butter or margarine.
2. Stack on the other ingredients. Add salt and pepper to taste.

Serves 2.

a coin inside the pudding, which is believed to bring good luck to the finder. The pudding is served warm in England.

Australians have tweaked the tradition to suit their climate and lifestyle. Christmas pudding is more likely to be a cold treat here than a traditional hot dessert. Instead of steaming the pudding for hours, many Australian cooks chill it overnight in a refrigerator or freezer.

They often substitute fresh fruit for dried fruit, which they blend with ice cream, or chilled crumbled fruitcake and vanilla icing. They, too, usually slip a coin or a small token into the pudding. During the Australian gold rush in the late 19th century, a real gold nugget was often hidden in the pudding. But Australians do not have to find gold in their Christmas pudding to enjoy it. Cold Christmas pudding is a perfect treat on a hot summer day—rich, creamy, cold, and refreshing.

Festive Sandwiches

On other special occasions, such as birthday parties or afternoon tea parties, festive sandwiches are often served. These, too, have a distinctive Australian flavor. Australians like their sandwiches thin and delicate. They start with sliced white bread that is traditionally cut thinner and shorter than American bread. They cut all the crusts off, which makes the bread even smaller. Before a filling is added, the bread is always topped with a thin layer of butter or margarine. Sandwiches are always cut into dainty triangles. Cutting them into fourths diagonally does this.

What goes inside the sandwich depends on the cook. Australians eat anything and everything on sandwiches, including cold spaghetti. Among their favorites for any occasion is a **vegemite** sandwich.

Vegemite is a smooth, sticky, dark-brown paste made from yeast that is a by-product of beer brewing. It has a very salty, earthy flavor, which can be overwhelming to non-Australians. "You either love it, or you hate it,"[15]

Australians put anything they want on sandwiches. Vegemite sandwiches are very popular. Vegemite is a smooth, sticky dark brown paste made from yeast that people either love or hate.

explains chef Melissa Plotkin.

Most Australians love it. According to Australian chef Sharon Robards, "if there is only one food that defined Australians, it would be vegemite. We love it! It is part of our identity and embedded into our culture."[16] For parties, Australians often serve open-style vegemite sandwiches. This means they use only one slice of bread, which they like to toast. They spread it with a thin layer of butter topped with an equally thin layer of vegemite. Some cooks add a slice of tomato.

Others prefer to serve tomato sandwiches. These

Fairy Bread

Fairy bread is easy and fun to make. If you want to be creative, you can mix chocolate sprinkles with colored sprinkles.

Ingredients
4 slices of bread
soft margarine
1/8 cup of colored sprinkles

Instructions
1. Spread the margarine on the bread. Be sure to cover all the bread so that the sprinkles will stick.
2. Cover the bread with sprinkles.
3. Cut the bread into fourths diagonally.
Serves 4.

are closed sandwiches made with thinly sliced tomato sprinkled with salt and pepper. Other popular sandwich fillings include asparagus spears, cucumbers, apples and raisins, sardines, or boiled eggs and lettuce.

Fairy bread, another unique Australian creation, is especially popular at children's parties. It consists of a slice of buttered white bread dusted with brightly colored candy sprinkles called **hundreds and thousands**, which stick to the butter. The bread is cut into triangles and stacked on a platter. With its dainty appearance, rainbow colors, and soft sugary taste, it is not hard to imagine this treat being consumed by tiny fairies or by happy Australian children. WoyWoy,

an Australian woman explains, "Fairy bread always brings fond memories. . . . [It was] always served at my children's birthday parties. Now adults, my son and daughter still ask for fairy bread."[17]

Special foods like fairy bread help create special memories. Australians love to have fun. Getting together with friends and family to celebrate holidays and special occasions is a vital part of Australian life. Adding festive foods such as Pavlova, White Christmas, creamy chilled puddings, and tasty little sandwiches makes these events all the more fun and memorable.

Metric conversions

Mass (weight)

1 ounce (oz.)	= 28.0 grams (g)
8 ounces	= 227.0 grams
1 pound (lb.) or 16 ounces	= 0.45 kilograms (kg)
2.2 pounds	= 1.0 kilogram

Liquid Volume

1 teaspoon (tsp.)	= 5.0 milliliters (ml)
1 tablespoon (tbsp.)	= 15.0 milliliters
1 fluid ounce (oz.)	= 30.0 milliliters
1 cup (c.)	= 240 milliliters
1 pint (pt.)	= 480 milliliters
1 quart (qt.)	= 0.96 liters (l)
1 gallon (gal.)	= 3.84 liters

Pan Sizes

8- inch cake pan	= 20 x 4-centimeter cake pan
9-inch cake pan	= 23 x 3.5-centimeter cake pan
11 x 7-inch baking pan	= 28 x 18-centimeter baking pan
13 x 9-inch baking pan	= 32.5 x 23-centimeter baking pan
9 x 5-inch loaf pan	= 23 x 13-centimeter loaf pan
2-quart casserole	= 2-liter casserole

Temperature

212° F	= 100° C (boiling point of water)
225° F	= 110° C
250° F	= 120° C
275° F	= 135° C
300° F	= 150° C
325° F	= 160° C
350° F	= 180° C
375° F	= 190° C
400° F	= 200° C

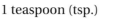

Length

1/4 inch (in.)	= 0.6 centimeters (cm)
1/2 inch	= 1.25 centimeters
1 inch	= 2.5 centimeters

Chapter 1: Nature's Bounty

1. Graeme Newman, *The Down Under Cookbook*, Albany, New York: Harrow and Heston, 1987, p. 44.

2. LifeTips, "Australian Fish and Chips," LifeTips, http://australian.lifetips.com/cat/59206/australian-food/index.html.

3. Quoted in Australis, "Australian Celebrity Chef Luke Mangan," Australis, www.thebetterfish.com/our-barramundi/spotlight/spotlight/australian-celebrity-chef-luke-mangan#idrckkgkrmg1laec9c3kau7aluke.

4. Quoted in *The Food of Australia*, Victoria, Australia: Periplus, 1996, p. 7.

5. Melissa Plotkin, interview with the author, March 20, 2009.

Chapter 2: Casual Living

6. Plotkin, interview with the author.

7. Betsey Newman and Graeme Newman, *Good Food from Australia*, New York: Hippocrene, 1997, p. 52.

8. Priscilla Cox, "Barbie Is a Great Cook," Oztralia.tv, March 7, 2008, http://blog.oztralia.tv/tag/cooking-in-australia.

9. Quoted in *The Food of Australia*, p. 22.

10. Newman and Newman, *Good Food from Australia*, p. 71.

Chapter 3: Delicious Snacks

11. Colin, interview with the author, March 7, 2009.

12. Woz, "ANZAC Biscuits," Aussie Slang, www.aussieslang .com/features/anzac-biscuits.asp.

13. Syrie Wongkaew, "Iconic Australian & New Zealand Foods," About.com, http://australianfood.about.com/od/ discoveraussienzfood/a/Iconicfoods.htm

Chapter 4: Foods for Holidays and Celebrations

14. Shuna Fish Lydon, "Pavlova," Simply Recipes, March 20, 2007, www.elise.com/recipes/archives/004356pavlova.php.

15. Plotkin, interview with the author.

16. Sharon Robards, "Vegemite," Australian Flavour, November 8, 2007, http://australianflavour.net/index. php?option=com_content&task=view&id=31&Itemid=1.

17. WoyWoy, "Cook's Profile," allrecipes.com, November 3, 2006, http://allrecipes.com/cook/1453773/profile.aspx.

Glossary

Aborigines: Australia's first inhabitants.

ANZAC: An acronym for the Australian New Zealand Army Corps.

aquaculture: Raising fish for food.

barbie: An Australian term for a barbecue grill.

barramundi (bar-a-mund-i): A fish caught in Australian waters and raised on Australian fish farms.

billy: A tin can that early Australian settlers used as a pot for cooking over a campfire.

biscuits: The Australian name for cookies.

bush tucker: Foods native to Australia.

canteen: A cafeteria in a school or business where food can be purchased.

cattle station: A cattle ranch.

chips: An Australian term for fried potatoes. Americans know them as French fries.

fairy bread: Bread topped with butter and candy sprinkles.

hundreds and thousands: The Australian name for candy sprinkles.

Lamingtons: Popular pastries made from sponge cake, chocolate, and coconut.

meringue (mer-rang): A delicate sweet made from egg white and sugar.

Moreton Bay bug: A type of small spiney lobster.

passion fruit: A tropical fruit that looks like a plum filled with seeds.

Pavlova: A meringue dessert named after the famous Russian ballerina Anna Pavlova.

prawns: Extra large shrimp.

scones (sconz): The Australian name for biscuits.

snags: An Australian term for sausages.

vegemite: A smooth, sticky, dark-brown paste made from brewer's yeast.

yabbies: Freshwater crayfish

For Further Exploration

Books

Erinn Banting, *Australia: The Culture*. New York: Crabtree, 2002. This book talks about Australian culture, including a section on food.

Mel Freidman, *Australia and Oceania*. New York: Children's Press, 2009. Facts about Australian landforms, animals, culture, and climate with statistics, photographs, and maps.

Elizabeth Germaine and Ann L. Burckhardt, *Cooking the Australian Way*. Minneapolis, MN: Lerner, 2003. This is an Australian cookbook for children.

Bobbie Kalman, *Spotlight on Australia*. New York: Crabtree, 2008. Interesting facts about life in Australia.

Miriam Lamb, *Australia*. Chicago: Heinemann Raintree, 2007. Facts about Australia's geography, wildlife, and people.

Web Sites

Aussie Cooking (www.aussiecooking.com.au). This Web site offers dozens of recipes for Australian foods.

Australia, CIA World Fact Book (https://www.cia.gov/library/publications/the-world-factbook/geos/

as.html). This website gives maps and facts about Australia's geography, people, economics, and government. It also has photographs and a picture of an Australian flag.

Australian Government Culture Portal (http://www .culture.gov.au/). This website provides a wealth of information about every aspect of Australia, including great pictures, links, stories for kids, and information about food and culture.

DLTK's Growing Together (www.dltk-kids.com). This Web site offers craft ideas and printable coloring pages for children. The "Countries and Cultures" section provides lots of information about Australia, including links to recipes and fun craft activities.

Pocantico Hills School, "Australia for Kids" (http:// www.pocanticohills.org/australia/australia.htm). Information about Australia researched and written by American middle school students.

Index

Aborigines, 19, 42

ANZAC biscuits, 34–36, *35*

ANZAC Day, *34*, 36

Aquaculture, 14

Arnott's Tim Tams, *31*, 32

Asian influences, 25

Aussie burgers, 8

Australia

food regions, *2*

history, 4, 6

language, 33

lifestyle, 17–18

natural resources, 4

wildlife, 9

Australian New Zealand

Army Corps, 34, *34*

Barbecuing

Australian lifestyle, 17–18

backyard barbies, *18*

history of, 18–20

mixed grill, 23, 25

prawns, *24*, 26

snags, 20, *20*, 22–23

Barramundi, *11*, 12, 14

Beef, 7–8, 25

Birds, 9

Biscuits and scones, *31*,
31–32, 34–36, *35*

Bread, 21, 48, 50–51

Breakfast, 44

Burgers, 8

Cakes, 36–37, *37*, *38*, 39

Cattle, 6–8

Cattlemen, 19

Celebrations, 41, 48–50

Children, 50–51

Chips, 23, *26*, 27–28

Christmas foods

Christmas pudding, 45,
46, 47–48

Pavlova, 43–45

preparation, 41–42

White Christmas, 42–43

Christmas pudding, 45,
46, 47–48

Colonial Australia, 4, 6, 42

Conversions, metric, 52
Convicts, 4, 6
Cookies. *See* Biscuits and
  scones

Damper, 21
Dinner, 44

Elizabeth II, Queen, 6
English, 33
Explorers, 6

Fairy bread, 50–51
Fast-food, 39–40
Feed for livestock, 7–8, 10
Fish, 10–12, *11*, 14, *26*
Fish-and-chips, *26*, 27–28
Fish farms, 14
Floaters, 40
Food regions of Australia,
  2
French fries. *See* Chips
Fruits, 14–16, *15*

Greek influences, 25

Hamburgers, 8
History
  Aboriginal culture, 42
  ANZAC biscuits, 34

barbecuing, 18–20
  colonial Australia, 4, 6
Hunting, 19, 42

Immigrant influences, 25

Kangaroos, 19

Lamb, 10, 25
Lamingtons, 36–37, *38*
Language, 33
Length conversions, 52
Lifestyle, 17–18
Liquid volume conver-
  sions, 52
Lunch, 44

Macadamia nuts, 30, *30*
Mammals, 9
Maps, *2*
Mass conversions, 52
Meals, 44
Measurement, 52
Meat
  beef, 7–8
  lamb, 10
  mixed grill, 25
  snags, 20, *20*, 22–23
  Toad-in-the-Hole, 13, *13*
Meat pies, *39*, 39–40

Men and barbecuing,
  22–23
Meringue, 43
Metric conversions, 52
Mixed grill, 23, 25
Moreton Bay bugs, 12

National Lamington Day,
  39
Native Australians. *See*
  Aborigines
Nuts, 30, *30*

Outback, 42
Outdoor cooking. *See* Bar-
  becuing
Outdoor eating, 26–28
  See also Barbecuing

Pan sizes, 52
Parades, *34*
Passion fruit, 14–15
Pastries, 39–40
Pavlova, *43*, 43–45
Pavlova, Anna, *43*, 45
Potato salad, 22
Prawns, 12, *24*, 26

Ranches. *See* Stations

Recipes
  ANZAC Biscuits, 35
  Aussie burger, *8*
  damper, 21
  Fairy bread, 50
  Lamingtons, 38
  potato salad, 22
  Salad Roll, 47
  Toad-in-the-Hole, 13

Salad roll, 47
Sandwiches, *44*, 47, 48–50,
  49
Sausage, 13, *13*, 20, *20*,
  22–23
Scones. *See* Biscuits and
  scones
Seafood, 10–12, 14, *24*, 26
Settlers, colonial, 4, 6
Sheep, 6–7, *7*
Shepherds, 19
Snacks
  ANZAC biscuits, 34–36,
    35
  Arnott's Tim Tam, *31*
  biscuits and scones,
    31–32
  cakes, 36–37, *38*, 39
  Lamingtons, 36–37, *38*

meat pies, *39*, 39–40
morning tea, 29–31
nuts, *30*
Snags, 20, *20*, 22–23, 25
Stations, 6–7, *7*
Summertime, 41

Takeaway food, 26–28
Tea breaks, 29–31
Temperature conversions, 52
Tim Tams, *31*, 32
Toad-in-the-Hole, 13, *13*

Tomato sandwiches, 49–50

Vegemite sandwiches, 48–49, *49*
Veterans, *34*
Volume conversions, liquid, 52

Weight conversions, 52
White Christmas, 42–43
Wildlife, 9
World War I, 34

Picture Credits

About the Author

Barbara Sheen is the author of more than 50 books for young people. She lives in New Mexico with her family. In her spare time, she likes to swim, walk, garden, and read. Of course, she loves to cook!